*Dis!*Organize

*Dis!*Organize:

An Intrapreneur's Guide To Making A Bigger Difference At Work.

Jonathan Anthony

Dedication

For all those who put up with my *"what if...?"* ideas and experiments over the years; and who encouraged my curiosity and push for more. *Salut*.

And for Lori, always and in every way.

Table of Contents

0: Preface

OK. Let's begin. Let's disorganize...

A few years ago, I read a *Fast Company* article[1] about the kinds of jobs people might have in 2025. One in particular caught my eye: a ***Corporate Disorganizer***, someone

> "who can introduce a little 'organized chaos', act more like a start-up, innovate and tap into new systems of the collaborative economy."

Yep. I like it. Does that sound like you too?

I started using an alternative job title that day, to better express the 'edge stuff' I was doing at work. Since then, I have learned a lot, and I have the bruises to prove it.

And now I am going to share it all with you –

99 simple tips, tricks, ideas and encouragements that make up ***An Intrapreneur's Guide to Making a Bigger Difference at Work.***

Each chapter is a single concept that can be read in 60 seconds, activated immediately, shared easily, and perfected over a lifetime of playing a bigger game at work.

There are always 99 problems...We are *not* one of them. Indeed, we can use any or all of these 99 prompts and insights to deliver outsize intrapreneurial outcomes for our organization; and get any stakeholder to "*Yes!*"

Bonne chance!

P.S.

If any of the ideas herein resonate with you, I have made a 60-second video version of every chapter, all 99 of which can be found here:
www.ThisMuchWeKnow.net/Disorganize

Please share the content freely with your own network.

I am always happy to discuss how intrapreneurs disorganize. I can be reached on various social channels:

Twitter: @ThisMuchWeKnow
LinkedIn: /in/ThisMuchWeKnow
Instagram: @Dis.Organize

Vancouver, Canada
August, 2020.

1: What's In A Name...?

Hello, I'm Jonathan and I'm a corporate disorganizer. Pleased to meet you.

What do you call yourself, when you decide to let loose in your organization to deliver MAXIMUM value?

Do you just say,

"Hello, I'm <insert NAME NAME> and I am a <insert BORING JOB TITLE HERE>"?*

Because that job title probably has an asterisk attached to it; and in the conversational footnote there is an explanation of this other 'thing' you do, this value you add, this approach you are practicing...

You need to name that asterisk. It needs its own business card. Everyone has a personal *shtick*. Name it, so that others have total recall why you should be in that meeting, on that project.

What nomenclature to use, to identify your unique brand of genius? *Change agent, rebel, disruptor, intrapreneur? Disorganizer?* Sure, all good.

But NAME it. Say it out loud. Disorganize.

2: Creative Destruction

The term "entrepreneurship" was first defined in 1942 by the economist Joseph Schumpeter, and its definition is utter genius:

creative destruction!

Schumpeter argued that progress occurs in 'cracks and leaps' not 'infinitesimal small steps.'[2]

Daniel Isenberg, the author of *Worthless, Impossible, and Stupid*, says:

> Entrepreneurs are contrarian value creators. They see economic value where others see heaps of nothing.

Well, hello there, corporate disorganizer! We absolutely see potential in creative destruction, in change and renewal, even in heaps of nothing. We possess the spark, the ignition for progress 'leaps'.

Corporate disorganizers are *intra*preneurs – we create anew inside the organization what the entrepreneur might outside, in the marketplace.

Here's to us, here's to the disorganizers!

3: Upset And Disorganize

So you now know the original – Joseph Schumpeter – definition of entrepreneurship:

> creative destruction!

Now, let's jump ahead in time, to the most famous management consultant of all – Peter Drucker.

In his seminal textbook on the subject, *Innovation and Entrepreneurship: Practice and Principles*, Drucker writes:

> [Schumpeter's definition of entrepreneurship] was intended as a manifesto and as a declaration of dissent: the entrepreneur ***upsets and disorganizes***.

kaBOOM!

Inside your organization, there is no time to lose. To make a difference, one must dissent the status quo, and sow the seeds of the organizational rebirth.

It's time to upset, and disorganize, no?

4: Creative Tension

As a communicator, I like this little bit of organizational physics:

> for each action there is an equal and opposite reaction (and a social media overreaction).

If you want to change what goes on around you in the workplace, you can expect pushback, so you need to embrace it, to use it as an activator.

Consciously introduce and manage the creative tension around you.

Prod and poke, push and withdraw, feeling the force of your boss, your team, and the organization in interplay with you.

It is a dance.

This is not about being a bull in a china shop. [Sadly, if you are a white middle aged man like me, that can work].

Seth Godin talks about **pattern interrupt**: we've been trained to ignore consistent, obvious messages and invocations - like the airplane seatbelt video.

If you want to cut through, you need to make a cut. Force those around you to notice, to play.

A healthy tension. A *creative* tension.

5: Disorganize The Job Description

Have you ever experienced this conundrum?

When you have a brilliant idea but you can't reach it from your job description.

Just. Out. Of. Reach.

Two choices:
> Keep reaching in the hope of growing longer arms; or
> Dig out your job description, open the doc, and tab to edit mode.

This goes for people in your team too. If you want to engage and retain "talent", create the opportunity for people to enjoy their damn jobs.

- Play to people's strengths
- Understand people as individuals
- Match their passion to the possibility
- Co-create what might be next
- Customize a career for them.

Help them create a role that has never existed before but that needs to be in your organization; that needs to be in the world.

And do it for yourself too.

#Disorganize!

6: Meander
(Hither And Thither)

Meander.

It's a great word. It just sounds right.

I first came across the word studying geography at school. A river meanders, gently swerving this way and that; the water slowly removing and depositing the earth of its banks as it moves inexorably to its destination. By doing so, it changes itself.

People should meander too. Hither and thither.

Of course, having direct line of sight to your career goal is Coolio. No distractions, go get it. Like an arrow.

But not 24-7.

You should reserve some space, some time, for more random adventures, experiments, and conversations. Go for a walk without a destination; meet a colleague or acquaintance for coffee without purpose. Noodle on a problem with a blank sheet of paper and some colouring pencils. And colour outside the lines.

Meander. Let the world surprise you with new intentions, new opportunities.

That's how we disorganize.

7: Context
(Which Side Is Right?)

My wife and I both sleep on the right side of the bed. It's not literally as weird as it sounds, but figuratively, it is.

My "right side of the bed" is the perspective from looking at the bed upon entering the room.

Her "right side" is from lying in bed looking out to the world.

We are both "right" about the "right side." It depends on our context.

There are very few agreed upon truths in our worlds. [Even seemingly obvious ideas like social justice, #BLM, and COVID-response...]

We rely heavily on context. In our workplaces, just as in our communities, that context is agreed upon by those who came before. But it is not necessarily "truth."

If we, as intrapreneurs and disorganizers, as agitators and protestors, seek to change the context, we must unstitch the "right side" of those who went before, piece by piece.

Godspeed!

8: 40% Sell

According to the author Daniel Pink in *To Sell Is Human*, we spend 40% of our time selling.

40% of our time...selling!

Work in an office and sit at a computer all day working on projects? Where is the selling?

In the craft of your emails; in the project updates in team meetings; in the deliverables of your projects; in the poise of your demeanour on the team Zoom call.

Always. Be. Selling.

If that 40% figure is correct, by god, we had better believe in something. We need to create meaning around us, or else it will be a struggle. Selling something you are not committed to, or have no interest in – good luck with that.

Disorganizing doesn't only mean changing things around you – it also means changing your own dynamic so that you always have a positive angle into the work. If you have that intrapreneurial mindset, selling is easy.

9: Power Pose

You have probably heard about the psychology behind the power pose.

Before an important meeting or a job interview; go into the bathroom and look at yourself in the mirror while standing powerfully, arms and legs akimbo, like the star you are. Take some deep breaths.

By doing so, you instill physical self-belief at the cellular level. You release endorphins of control and confidence. You establish your force field.

Now you can go out into the world and disorganize!

Others will believe you, believe me.

Go get 'em.

P.S.: Want to go NEXT LEVEL on this? Maybe repeat a mantra to yourself too:

Yes, yes, YES!

But be careful you don't spontaneously combust in your own vibrant intrapreneurial magnificence!

10: *"Dis-...!"* Your Company

So I call myself a corporate disorganizer and an intrapreneur.

I could call myself, and sometimes do, a change agent, rebel, a disruptor.

Why "disorganizer?"

Well, a disorganizer is unexpected, it comes from a side angle, it slows the recipient down. It opens up a conversation.

> *"But, I'm not disorganized!"*

you say. Exactly right.

I am not *disorganized*, passive, careless and undisciplined.

I <u>*disorganize*</u>, active verb:

> "disrupt the systematic order or functioning of..."

Dis- is a Latin prefix meaning apart, asunder, away, utterly...

"Disrupt" has been claimed as a force of good in the workplace economy.

> *"Disrupt or be disrupted!"*

Its overuse has made it almost meaningless. Why not "disorganize" instead? Do you work for an organization that doesn't need *Dis*-ing?!

11: ACT!

The great Chinese artist, dissident and provocateur Ai Wei Wei says:

> My favourite word is ACT.
>
> I am more fearful than other people, maybe, then I act more brave because I know the danger is really there. If you don't act, the dangers become stronger.

Now, at work we can come to action from both perspectives:
Fear – that, if we do not have the courage to take control of our own destiny, we will instead be inserted into some maelstrom of nonsense; or
Optimism and opportunity – that, by rolling up our sleeves and moving out into the world, we will create magic.

Either way, my protestation is – *do the work.*

Have **a bias towards action**. Be creative, have ideas, but put them into action, or else it's just fluff.

The more we take action, the more fun we can have with it. The more memories we create; the more we have to show for our valour and commitment; the more disorganizing we put into effect.

12: Pay It Forward

In the last chapter, Ai Wei Wei showed us that taking action requires bravery. That courage builds muscle. It gives us a force field.

Hey, we're still here...we disorganizers have been (at least partially) successful. If we weren't, we would have already been shown the door. We have good instincts. Now, we must pay it forward.

The ability to effect change, the intrapreneurial effort you introduce, can be shared with others.

We can pay it forward to that friend, colleague, or onlooker who wants to similarly make a difference but who has yet to build up the confidence to deliver on their genius (idea), with the confidence and fidelity required to get traction.

They need partners in crime. They need confidants, supporters, sounding boards.

They need disorganizers.

And so do we.

13: Work Out Loud

To disorganize your company is to activate change, releasing new, positive energy. However, if it is done in private, the energy is likely to be misplaced.

Change without narrative and community access and engagement generates whispers, gossip. It becomes too political, heavy with fear and suspicion.

> – *"what is s/he up to?"*;

The future of work should be
> observable; and
> narrated.

Work. Out. Loud. People need to see what you are up to, so you get rid of the politics. The work, the ideas are then exposed and transparent.

Then it needs to be explained and discussed; such that you can get the feedback you need to test, iterate, refine, and to fail (forward).

Working out loud allows intrapreneurs to include and enable the *hivemind*, and improve all actions and outcomes in unexpected directions.

#WOL #WorkOutLoud

14: Challenge Everything

Consider the organizational view. Maybe even author it, and believe in it.

Build and deliver the norms and processes that deliver against that view. That is *NORMAL*.

But! (There is always a *but*!)

Challenge *EVERYTHING*.[3]

Step outside the norm, determine its limitations, stress test its boundaries.

Begin to author the next version of the organization, as you deliver the current one.

Intrapreneurship is not about smashing the system. It is about evolving the new one.

15: Move to The Edge

When you are at the edge – of the ocean, of the cliff – you have a long horizon.

You can see for miles. You see the weather front rolling in. You see the change in conditions; you call to those behind you:

"Ahoy!"

The same is true inside your company.

You need the edge worker to forewarn, to paint a picture of how the world is changing.

Counter-intuitively to many leaders, this edge worker should be encouraged to move forward and away.

This means embracing a kind of cognitive dissonance: look for those who are moving in new directions, maybe even away from the organization, and see if that is your company's new tomorrow too.

#edgeworker

16: Blow Shit Up

Cindy Gallop[4] has the best twitter bio of all:

I like to blow shit up. I am the Michael Bay of business.

KaBOOM.

Gallop is redefining our collective approach to ageing, sextech, funding female founders, #changetheratio in advertising among other things. She fights for what she believes in. She is a hero to many, me included.

She cajoles:

"[D]on't *#leanin* within the existing system, redesign the system...The answer is not women trying to become more like men; the answer is men trying to become more like women."

This message is universal: those unheard voices and lesser debated ideas deserve their chance in the workplace. You will be rarely invited to opine or experiment as an outsider.

Sometimes, you need to redesign the system...you need to blow shit up.

17: Creativity As A Renewable Resource

When we disorganize our organization, we are rebirthing it, evolving it.

Evolution is full of examples of species that die in that act of procreation. Do we want to die in our process, in our commitment to our craft?

Hmmm, nope.

We want to prosper, alongside the corporate culture we are recreating.

Conundrum!

What do we therefore need? This tweet:

> Creativity is a renewable resource in courageous corporate cultures.

So written by my friend Lois Kelly[5]. It stopped me in my tracks (admittedly, I was just sitting on my sofa when I read it, but anyway...)

Creativity is a renewable resource in courageous corporate cultures. We must find those courageous cultures; or else, we must create them first.

Lois has done so over the years, as she grows wiser, wilder, kinder. She calls herself a *rebel at work*; but yeah, she's a disorganizer too.

18: Fork In The Road

You have probably heard of the famous Yogi Berry malapropism

> Whenever you come to a fork in the road, take it.

Ok, but, y'know, which way?

The right way, of course!

Ok, but, y'know, which way is that right way?

Well, it's time to make your own map. It's time to concoct your own story as you go. It's time to use your senses!

Intrapreneurs own it. They own their own lives; they are not waiting for others to show them the way. They are creating the correct way forward, bushwhacking as they go.

I'm off, to disorganize….um…this way.

19: We Become Seekers

When I became a parent, I had a reawakening of my curiosity gene. Watching my kids learn and experiment into the world was a magical moment in my life, one that I brought, whole, to work.

It reminded me of a favourite quote, by the explorer and author Peter Matthiessen:

> "Soon the child's clear eye is clouded over…
>
> Not until years later does an instinct come that a vital sense of mystery has been withdrawn.
>
> The sun glints through the pines and the heart is pierced in a moment of beauty and strange pain, like a memory of paradise. After that day, *we become seekers*."

The worker we all need to be, the worker that every company needs, is a seeker.

Stay curious, disorganizer!

20: EMPTY! <Insert Topic Here>

I have been sharing the ABCDEs of disorganizing your workplace - a bunch of action, bits and bytes of knowledge, concepts, definitions and encouragements.

But here is where I pause for a moment and leave some space.

What is your idea, your exploration, your good intent? What is your experiment, or your book of choice insights?

> Write it down.
> Describe it.
> NOW SHARE IT WITH SOMEONE!!

Over coffee, at the watercooler, on the team Zoom meeting, at the party where everyone is more "relaxed"...

Put it out into the world.

> "Ideas that spread, win"

says Seth Godin.

Let's manufacture our own win. Let's disorganize.

21: Emergence

There is not that much in the workplace that is simple. Those best practices, that are obvious to all, may get us through the day but will probably not meet tomorrow's needs.

For that, we need to embrace a more complex approach, of emergent practices.

And here's the thing about complexity: the relationship of cause and effect can only be seen in hindsight. What works can only be seen in the rear view mirror.

We must probe, sense, then respond.

Complexity should be ridden like a beast, because it cannot be stick handled and process managed. Emergence prepares us for a more uncertain, chaotic tomorrow.

Organizationally, therefore, we should seek out and reward different cultural contributors: misfits and original thinkers who stretch and enrich[6], those who play in complexity.

Y'know, intrapreneurs.

22: Share Is The New Save

You create a document, a piece of content or data or design. You hit the floppy disk icon and save it to a drive. You email it to a few people. You decide who needs to know what and when.

This is about control.

But here's the thing:

> The world is moving too fast for us to control every step and process and data point.

Our networks – internal and external – are pulsing with information and knowledge and expertise. Better quality knowledge and expertise and help than we have in our own domain.

We need to embrace this network opportunity. We need to share.

This should be the default position we take with our data, our knowledge. Share openly, as widely as possible (like this book!).

Work out loud. Disorganize through collaboration and engagement. Let the network in.

Share is the new save.

23: Learn, Unlearn, Relearn

Futurist Alvin Toffler had it right when he said:

> "The illiterate of the 21st century will not be those who cannot read and write, but those who cannot learn, unlearn, and relearn."

This is the fluency we all need as workers.

And here's the thing, all adult learning is optional. We need to make a choice.

Intentionality creates the environment where people can develop.

The great future of worker thinker Harold Jarche refines this idea as:

> *Work is learning and learning is the work*[7].

Intrapreneurs get this. It is in their bones. Does your organization get it too? If not, hire some unlearners, relearners, some disorganizers!

24: Kith And Kin (Insiders)

Many people will not get you at work – guaranteed. They'll roll their eyes; make some gentle joke at your expense. Maybe you will be politically sidelined.

Two choices:
> Time for a new job (*yep!*); or
> Scan the company for those fellow travellers who do, or might, get you.

Who has quirks, ideas, musings that sit outside the organizational norm? Who is an outcast? Not the deadwood stuck in the past but the weirdo clearly living in the future?

- Say hi.
- Go for coffee.
- Comment and like their contributions on the social network.
- Ask for their advice or input.

Strength in numbers, emotional support, fellow travellers...

We cannot disorganize alone.

25: Kith And Kin (Outsiders)

Here's another guarantee: there are people just like you, trying to do the same work – in other organizations.

Nothing you are doing is unique (*sorry*).

And! Guaranteed! Some of these people will be way ahead of you on the journey.

They have the bruises and trips and falls. They have the victories, small and sweet. And they are willing to share – indeed, they want to get it off their chest with someone who might get them.

So join a community, go to a meet-up, sign up for a MOOC; find out who else is using your vendor's tool and reach out.

Find your fellow travellers, your fellow disorganizers.

26: Pick Yourself

The last couple of chapters I have been talking about how to find others who can help you be successful.

But here's the thing: it *is* down to you.

No-one is going to rescue you from the bubble of your own good ideas.

Here I'm going to defer to that great marketer and explainer about how to make a difference, Seth Godin[8]:

> "The ultimate privilege is to pick ourselves. To decide that the most important person to be chosen by is our self.
>
> If you pick yourself as the chooser, if you give yourself the power to say 'go', I hope you'll respect how much power you have, and not waste it."

Gulp.

Disorganizers intuitively understand that it is their turn - to stand for something, to make the bigger difference.

To pick ourselves.

27: L.A.M.S.T.A.I.H.

LAMS-TAY - *Look. At. More. Stuff. Think. About. It. Harder.*

This is a call to action for all disorganizers.

Don't phone it in at work. Create the new, the next, the better version.

It requires open eyes, an open mind, and an open heart. It means working harder at the inputs.

You need to see the same old, same old with fresh eyes, fresh possibilities. And you need fresh, new inputs too.

Look at more stuff...

You need to put yourself in unusual situations, maybe difficult ones.

- Go for a walking meeting; take photos of esoteric things.
- Gather a bunch of weird and wonderful post-it notes from your team about a topic.
- Read a book with a pencil in one hand and scribble marginalia.

Then, *think about it harder...*

Make a new map of the terrain. Experiment. Fail forward.

Disorganize.

28: Create A Manifesto

Create a manifesto!

Manifesto is defined as:

> "a published verbal declaration of the intentions, motives, or views of the issuer. Promotes a new idea with prescriptive notions for carrying out changes the author believes should be made."

Manifesto sounds a bit too much, a bit too far? I get it. Then try a credo instead.

Credo is Latin for

> *"I believe..."*

A credo is your own belief system through which you move out into the world to make a difference and disorganize.

If you believe, it *will* be enough.

29: Keep Calm; (Don't) Carry On

In pandemic times, it's good to follow the advice from that well-known Wartime reminder that people have pinned up in their workstation:

KEEP CALM AND CARRY ON.

In our workplace, however, we should take more care, and question our surroundings more critically. If your organization has been working remotely during COVID, we know that everything changes, and we are not going back to normal.

The new normal that emerges will be different. We will NOT carry on as before.

However, we will handle those changes, big or small, with a clear eye, a deep breath, and a kind smile.

Intrapreneurs keep calm, but don't carry on.

30: Curiosity Is The Killer App

Everything around change should start with curiosity:

> Who are we?
> How did we get here?
> Where are we heading?
> Are there other options for us?
> *Oooh*! What's that?
> Tell me more!

Curiosity is the base ingredient for learning; which, as our kids showcase to us daily, is the critical component of adaptability, growth, change and potentiality.

Now, add in some confidence and you have a winning recipe. A confidence that says,

> I think I can move forward.
> Progress is in my control.
> I have options here.
> I can add value.

[BTW: it's not about ego and being right and better than everyone else.]

Confidence + curiosity = creativity.

And creativity is about the only thing currently holding back our killer robot overlords.

Be creative. Be confident. Be curious. This is the disorganizer's credo.

31: The Edge Is The New Core

Traditionally, inside a company, you want to be an insider. Close to the action, in the oak-panelled room, smelling the power…

You listen closely for the organizational narrative and make sure you always onside with the guy in the corner office.

These days, not so much…

Increasingly, there is more value at the edge of the organization. The edge worker is not stuck in the bubble of orthodoxy. She sees more clearly what's around us, what's coming up behind us.

The edge worker is more likely to be connected to external people, industry leaders, more connected into the zeitgeist, more in tune with what is happening in the emergent world.

The intrapreneur embraces the idea:

the edge is the new core[9].

32: Sturgeon's Law

The science fiction writer Theodore Sturgeon famously said:

"Ninety percent of everything is crap.**"**

This became known as Sturgeon's Law, and it is applied to the advantage of the disorganizer.

Everyone else makes outsize promises about their work, they ask for the big budgets and large teams.

Still, they fail in their plans and quests...90% of the time.

We all know it to be true. How often do we say of an organizational project, product, roll-out or strategy,

"Nailed it!"?

Maybe 10% of the time, right?

The disorganizer, however, avoids this hubris:

- Fail forward with intent.
- Challenges all assumptions.
- Share and get feedback.
- Place small bets; and join the dots accordingly.

So what is 90% of everything is crap!? The disorganizer embraces Sturgeon's Law. No sweat.

33: Coffee-A-Go-Go

The value of network effects has been proven in workplaces.

The more interconnected we are, the more likely it is that projects will succeed, that institutional muscle memory grows.

There are many ways to grow organizational networks, and here's one experiment!

On your social network or in your office, start a coffee dating service. Random people put their name forward, with the intent to meet new colleagues and grow their network.

You simply connect those random people from different departments or floors to others, and invite them to get coffee.

No direction, no agenda. Just ask good questions, become better acquainted, understand each other better.

It's time to coffee-a-go-go!

P.S.
It's a nice touch to formally sponsor the initiative and get the company to pay for the coffee; but my advice.. don't ask HR. Just do it, unofficially.

If you have questions, I can share more disorganizer details on how to do it.

34: Give A FUQ!

You have heard of FAQs – *frequently asked questions*.

Something is happening in your organization and you need to explain it all to a stakeholder group.

The answers tend to be factual and dull. Anyone who has done media training will know how to stick to the line.

What about FUQs? *Frequently UNASKED questions*.

These are the things going on in your mind, in the minds of your team, the questions and conversations that get discussed when no-one else is watching.

Not the lame-ass one floated at the all-hands town hall meeting.

Disorganizers give a FUQ.

They are ahead and prepared for the tough conversations around challenge and change.

They are ready.

35: Fail Forward

Start small, make the kind of mistakes where you can exclaim *"Oopsie!"* and everyone lets you get on with cleaning up the mess.

Make another mistake – but never the same one. (That gets you escorted out of the door.)

Make a new mistake, based on the learning you made previously.

Example:

In safety workplaces, "near miss" reporting is an excellent example of learning by doing, failing forward. Every time something could have gone wrong, it is reported. The more reports made, the more the team is rewarded.

The alternative is

> *"Nothing to see here! Everything's ok!"*

The result of which: catastrophe, sometime, not sure when, we just know it will happen. The team will fall off the side of the cliff.

Show that there is growth in the process, share the process, learn as you disorganize – work out loud, right?

36: Everything Is Remix

One of the challenges of ego in the creative process is the idea that

"I have nothing unique to say!"

All that has ever been said or made is a click away. What value does my voice add?

Well, it turns out that nearly everything "unique" that has been said, or made, or created, is merely a facsimile of something that went before. Almost nothing is *truly* unique, spirited from the ether by a bold and mad genius.

Everything is remix.

Kirby Ferguson[10] made an amazing series of videos on this topic, which changed the way I looked at my own creative process.

He asserts there are three basic elements of creativity:

copy, transform, and combine.

With a juggle of these three components, you add, steal and launch things that already existed in new, emergent ways. There is no need to be unique; no requirement for genius. Just a genuine curiosity about what you can do.

Disorganizers remix.

37: Elevator Pitch

On the elevator ride to the 21st floor, a former CEO of mine would enquire about my family situation; and then recall it perfectly on each subsequent shared journey from reception.

We had a complete, tailored conversation in that claustrophobic shared space.

What question would you ask your CEO if the roles were reversed?

What small, precise story would you articulate? What perfectly played interaction would you manage in that 30-second private experience?

In life, you never know when the next opportunity will be to impress, to connect, to rattle the cage. You should be prepared.

Managing upwards, impressing with a *"What if...?"*, turning a stranger into an admirer. You might only have a moment to execute. Seize it.

This is an intrapreneur's stealth weapon, one that unlocks the budgets and projects and opportunities to act.

38: 80:20

You get 80% of the way there with 20% of the effort.
You execute 80% of the deliverables with 20% of the team.
80% of the complaints come from 20% of the people.
80% of the value of the work is achieved with 20% of the actions.

You get the point. Very little we do needs to get to *100*.

Perfection is your enemy.
Over-promising is your downfall.
A large budget is your distraction.

Instead, imagine what 80% of your organizational dreams and aspirations look like. Aim there.

Keep things small - at 20%: your team, the monies spent, the promises made.

Then apply your intrapreneurial ideas and skills and create some organizational wow.

Where the hell did that come from?!

They won't know what hit them.

39: EFFICIENCY!

All well-respected corporate environments have a certain phraseology that says to the world:

> "We are professional and august."

One of the top 10 words, if you ever want to be the HIPPO - highest paid person in the room - is

> *"Efficiency."*

Even those who proclaim *"DISRUPTION!"* and *"CHALLENGE!"* on their start-up T-shirts often prefer some good ol' productivity and cost reduction outcomes.

Although the intrapreneur is not usually driven by such straightforward outcomes, we can play that game and win, every time.

Because by the very nature of how we create, test, iterate and scale, our disorganizing is usually low-cost; it is low-risk, high-reward; it should definitely under-promise and over-deliver.

The failures are low-key and undramatic. The wins can have an order of magnitude outcome.

We can use and own the word EFFICIENCY. Disorganizers can fit in.

40: We Lead!

Talking with organizational execs, one of their biggest conundrums is:

"Dead wood."

People around them without the same insights and ability to move the organization forward the way "they" can.

"If only there were more people who lead rather than manage...!"

[As an aside...I ain't saying that idea is right. My guess is that if leaders worked harder at unlocking each colleague's value, they might surprise themselves to find they ain't the smartest people in the room.]

But if you want people who lead...

Yes. Well. Hello.

We are here – disorganizers, intrapreneurs.

Leading beyond our title, without explicit permission. We do it because we have a passion for more and a twinkle in our eye. We lead ourselves.

Now let us help lead the organization forward too.

41: Shtick Options

I am noodling on an idea or project in the corner, under the radar. A little bit of testing, iteration...

I work out loud to get some feedback from the *hivemind* (internal and external).

Now, I want to raise the possibility more widely, maybe get some corporate buy-in. I start talking about it more widely, creating some shtick around it.

Test and iterate on the messaging too. Don't put all your eggs in one basket. Have a back-up plan for your initiative, and how you talk about it too.

Big Cheese Dude over here likes words like *"disruption"* and *"the future."* Meanwhile, the HIPPO Exec over there prefers *"Efficiency"* and *"customer service."* Got it.

Different framing for different stakeholders, all in service of avoiding *"No!"*; to get sponsors to *"Yes!"*

Companies segment their customers and services and investments. Inside big corporations, this is called "optionality."

Intrapreneurs need options too.

42: Umuntu Ngumuntu Ngabantu

There is a wonderfully elegant Zulu saying:

Umuntu Ngumuntu Ngabantu.

A person is a person because of people.

When I slow down and really contemplate that sentence I am transported out of my own head and into a shared reality that I am mutually creating with others.

A person is a person because of people.

Sometimes, trying to disorganize your company can seem rather a lonely undertaking. One small voice, often stuck in its own echo chamber, up against the behemoth bureaucracy bellowing its blandishments.

We need help, we need friends, we need other people, to support us, to encourage, to make us whole.

Disorganizers always look for the helpers, and let them help.

43: Antifragile

I like Nassim Nicholas Taleb's writing on antifragility. In his *Heuristics* paper, he shares the general principle of antifragility:

> **It is much better to do what you cannot explain, than explain what you cannot do.**

Ah, *snap.*

Now, I do a lot of things; but this book is, of course, somewhat of an explainer, so I am a bit stuck.

Forgive me, then, if I share a bit on how I do...

- Read widely, follow links and nodal pathways.
- Consume content, then curate and synthesize.
- Challenge my own assumptions.
- Iterate over formal plans.
- Plan through small tests, under the radar.
- Fail forward.
- Play the long game, but test every day.
- Push for more.
- Actively manage upwards.
- Stick to simple rules.
- Build in redundancy and layers so there is no single point of failure.
- Embrace serendipity.
- etc. etc. etc.

Disorganizers are *antifragile.*

44: C H A l l e N G E & C H A N G E

Challenge and change. The two go hand in hand.

We have an emergent challenge – and the only thing to do is to *change* something, maybe everything, to overcome it.

We want to change something. Oh, but by doing so, we have to *challenge* our assumptions, maybe our processes.

Hand in hand.

And lo, the first three and the last three letters of *CHALLENGE* spells *CHA-NGE*. Hand in hand.

The disorganizer is a natural change agent. *Check*.

The disorganizer never accepts the status quo; they seek that new challenge. *Check*.

You can't spell challenge without change.

I don't know about you, but every year of work for me has been full of challenge and change. That is partially a choice. I don't take the well-trodden path, I look for the one less travelled, for the bigger possible reveal at the end.

If you want something to change in your work life, then you need a challenge. Ask for one from your team or leader. If there is none to hand, create one instead. Take ownership of something.

Conversely, if you want a new challenge, you are going to have to change; or, at least, effect change in others. Probably both.

45: Go Public I: Email

People without organizational power but with great ideas need to get their message out.

If you hide yourself away, you might discover the elixir to organizational life and no-one would be better off.

Working out loud is what it's called. Sharing what you know or believe is how it's done.

How to so do?

Let's consider the enemy of the modern organization - email.

Email is about:
>   control - I decide who has access; and
>   waste - spamming data into someone's inbox who is neither interested nor invested.

It is also about missed opportunity. Who might want that data but is not cc'd?!

If you want to engage the right people at the right time, *#NoEmail* is something to consider. It is a commitment to working in the open.

I discovered the pursuit of #NoEmail from the online collaboration leader Luis Suarez[11], who has been at it for 20 years. He got down to 4-5 emails a week in his role as a global collaboration consultant at IBM.

There are people out there, ahead. Seek them out, ask for their advice.

46: Go Public II: ESN

In the last chapter, I complained about email's inability to scale.

It is good one-to-one; but there are always missed opportunities to connect the right people with the right content. Oftentimes, that means new people, new network connections.

@elsua developed his career by bravely moving his work and conversations into online, open spaces such as twitter and enterprise social networks (ESN).

Your ESN is a special place for ideas to ferment and catalyze into actions.

Share widely your disorganizer projects; find fellow travellers who are excited by the same practices and who can help you get there faster.

Guaranteed, in many of those endeavours, it will be strangers who help; or at least people with unexpected skills and interests.

Stop thinking you:
>   can do it alone; and
>   have to always work within the parameters of the delineated org
>   chart.

Disorganizers bravely go public with their work and interests, and let the network in through technology.

47: Identify Your Kryptonite

I once developed a big digital transformation presentation for my Executive team. I needed some wow factor; some edge thinking that would surprise them and stop them in their tracks.

BLOCKCHAIN!

It kicked off an interesting discussion that went from bamboozlement, to curiosity, investigation, then eventually to "finger quote marks" <*oooh, "blockchain"*> before being swept out the door as detritus.

I never formally mentioned it again.

Know your Kryptonite.

Know what idea or action or concept will kill your superpower in your organization.

You have worked hard to have influence, to get things done and be allowed to operate independently.

Be savvy.

Once you have been burned a couple of times in the experimentation phase, no matter how attracted to it you are, or how much you know you can do with it...

Don't touch it.

Sometimes, the best thing an intrapreneur can do is simply walk away...

48: Commiserate

Disorganizers have bruises from their fights and muscle from the experimentation and small victories.

We know how to make things happen and lead the emergent edge of the organizations we serve.

Because we have fallen down so many times (and got back up again) there is little that could happen to a colleague who is trying for change that we have never yet experienced.

Therefore, be a shoulder to cry on. We should commiserate.

This is not just because we understand the challenge, but because we had others in our network who did it for us when we started shaking the organizational tree.

For me it was the Change Agents Worldwide[12] network. That superstar cohort supported my growth; we pay it forward.

In the age of COVID, this will be even more important. There will be more workplace challenge and therefore more workers challenging assumptions and trying for more.

Disorganizers are here to help.

49: Modern Art

Modern art = I could do that + Yeah, but you didn't.

I like modern art.

I occasionally buy cheap pieces to hang on the wall. I like its wry appraisal of the world and its commitment to ideas.

Modern art is not about being the most technically "talented." It's about big, bold ideas, about creative tension.

Modern art is an alive conversation between the artist and the viewer. It has entertainment value; it is in search of the zeitgeist.

The most common comment on modern art is

> *"I could do that."*

And the perfect riposte is

> *"Yeah, but you didn't."*

Disorganizers understand this equation. Our work is not rocket science. Anyone can do it, but not everyone does.

Intrapreneurship is the work of the modern day artist.

50: How Can I Help?

Disorganizers will often be accused of messing things up, with their crazy ideas and fail forward activities. And it is often true - we seek to change the status quo.

The reflective question to consider is,

> Do things need to change?

If the answer is 'no', our interventions are probably more about us than better organizational outcomes.

All our ideas and actions should support, or give suggestions or answers to the question

> *"How can I help?"*

If the answer is *"In no way whatsoever,"* well, time to move on, or settle down.

Asking *"How can I help?"* puts the recipient in a position of reflection and power. They consider their worldview and guide you accordingly.

As an intrapreneur, whichever way they guide you is enough. You have the ideas and commitment to make it work.

51: Engineer, Don't Disrupt

"Disruption" can be a trope, a cliché. Its overuse makes it empty of meaning.

Be careful with your language, of how to describe your skills, your value add.

Look around and find a definition or title you like. Experiment with it, start by using it in lower case before it becomes 'a thing.'

Surrounded by people who don't like such edgy thinking? Well, rather than disorganizer or disruptor, how about "Organizational Engineer"?!

Sounds serious, more formal, right?

I saw this recruitment advert recently, looking for someone who is an

- Expert in new ways of working.
- Facilitator of virtual team effectiveness.
- Developer of all types of leadership.
- Expert at talent transitions.
- Master of task optimization and organization principles such as agility, networks, power and trust

Cool.i.o.

Disorganizer or engineer, pick your own descriptor, pick yourself.

Now, go out and change the world.

52: It Might Get Ugly

There is a simple graph that very well describes the experience of many intrapreneurs trying to make a bigger difference inside an organization.

On the X axis, your desk. On the Y axis, your head.

The graph shows an elegant, consistent motion between the two.

> *Head: Desk. Head: Desk.*

Life at the edge of your company can get pretty ugly. *Fugly*, even.

I often refer to the bruises and muscle building produced in the act of disorganizing. It is a physical endeavour.

It can also give you monumental headaches. The type you get from:

> a hangover (the victory!); or
> a migraine (when a storm is brewing); or
> banging your head against the desk (we persevere...)

No matter the pain, consider the gain. Disorganizers keep going.

53: Ask The CEO For Coffee

Breakthroughs usually require some bravery. The entrepreneur *"upsets and disorganizes"*, in the words of Peter Drucker.

How does the intrapreneur break through? Usually by using their wits and thinking outside the box.

Imagine you have "10 IDEAS TO CHANGE THE COMPANY." Some experiments and tests, discussion topics and low-cost, fail forward initiatives.

How to execute them?

> Ask your line manager stuck deep within the org chart to sponsor your programs. *Bleugh.*
> Book a meeting called "My 10 ideas that will change the company" and invite the C-Suite. *Wowzer.*
> Or, go above and beyond the hierarchical process - ask a C-Suiter for coffee.

Ask good questions; solicit some advice; chat about stuff. Leave behind some ideas, your intent and capacity.

Let your ideas and potential seep into the organization.

Hopefully, those ideas will become hers, and you can be her disorganizer. Why not?!

54: Have Fun

Please excuse the white male privilege in my workplace experience, but here goes...

Have fun at work!

If your focus is on the pain and not the gain, the politics and not the breakthroughs, then you can end up self-actualizing a vortex of doom and gloom that will suck the life force from your disorganizer soul.

[Sad face.]

Don't take your role too seriously. It is unlikely to be a matter of life and death.

Determine where you can play, where you can generate energy and flow.

Plant a smile on your face. It is contagious, and proven to make people think you are smarter than you are.

Breakthrough!

If you are having fun, you become more attractive; people want in on your initiatives; they listen to your shtick.

Who said work had to be so serious all the time? Call bullshit on the downers.

Have fun.

55: R.E.S.P.E.C.T.

R-E-S-P-E-C-T. Find out what it means to me...

Ah, Aretha. I feel ya. When she's singing,

"All I'm askin' is for a little respect (just a little bit)..."

I'm thinking,

"OK, how to go about getting some?"

By definition, an intrapreneur is trying to do more than they can achieve by their default place in the org hierarchy. The disorganizer is circumventing the situation in which they find themself.

How do you earn some respect beyond the role you occupy?

Turns out, there's some social science about respect [and - *trigger warning!* - it plays into the hands of the middle class, white male].

According to *Barking Up the Wrong Tree*[13], the killer combo for respect is **confidence and competence**.

For competence, simple: work hard and become an expert at your job. Competence breeds real confidence. It engenders a feeling of control, it kills fear. It gives you bearing...

Finally, sprinkle in some moderate *overconfidence* to garner the respect you feel is due. See the world accurately but have belief in your abilities. *Bingo.*

(**cough** white, male privilege.)

56: The Battle Is Everything

I used to walk past a window display that had a beautifully calligraphed message for the world:

All of my good ideas are battles...

I think about that sign often.

Not much that I do or achieve comes easily. There is a lot of thinking, reading and research, a lot of reimagining that goes into the work before it even begins.

Many experiments fail. They take too long, the tech does not deliver, the messaging misses the mark, people misunderstand my intent.

Fortunately, I have reactivated my learning instinct.

As I experiment and craft, part of me disassociates and starts observing. The learning comes from the syntheses, the reflection, the try again.

This gives the disorganizer weaponry for those battles of ideas and power and influence.

It is hard graft, but I believe that victory can be ours.

57: Work Backwards

I read Scott Anthony's *Little Book of Innovation*. He defines innovation as:

something different that has impact.

Sounds like a disorganizer's credo...

One of his ideas that really resonated with me was about working backwards:

> "Start with an answer and then work backwards to map out assumptions that need to be true for that answer to be plausible."

"*Work backwards.*"

Uncover a desire, unlock a learning, scan for an opportunity, align your ducks...only then, work out what it might mean, how to impart its power.

Not everything needs to be 'strategic.'

Produce something 'cold' to gauge reaction and learn about the process. Then, we go and sell. Then, we move to project sponsorship and production.

If we are agile and opportunistic, and cut ourselves some slack, intrapreneurs will unlock value.

Tomorrow is another day.

Footnote[14]: We grow strong through experimentation. Some activities we undertook for input and creative stretch included: mocking up a culture wall, jerryrigging a digital display, hosting open houses with open questions, running Pecha Kucha sessions...

58: Everyone Anytime Everywhere Anything

The designer Bruce Mau shared his Incomplete Manifesto for Growth[15] 20 years ago. It is a work that every intrapreneur needs. My favourite proclamation therein:

> Begin Anywhere.

OK then, I will.

The most exciting outcome of social media and so-called social business is that the political, commercial, social, philosophical conversation opened up, many to many, any to any, in all directions.

That conversation is for *everyone, at any time, everywhere, about anything.*

This is our opportunity. There is nothing out of scope.

Whatever it is that is on your mind, there are people out there waiting to hear from you, to join you on your quest. To make a difference. To disorganize and change the world.

Everyone, anytime, everywhere, anything.

[Or...*Anyone – every time – anywhere - everything.*]

Now is the time.

59: Self-Evident

Over the last decade I have been working in the personal branding space. My interest is in trying to move beyond the job description in activating my skills and those of my colleagues.

Calling myself a disorganizer is about saying "*I am more than a communications professional.*"

There is a clear need for this work. When I ask people what they are good at, there are usually two types of response.

Firstly, uncertainty, a lack of clarity.

Secondly, a sense of obviousness.

> *"Isn't it entirely clear?"*

No, it is not. It is rarely self-evident. Ambrose Bierce defines that term as,

> *"evident to oneself and no-one else."*

This is the work, friends.

So much value is left on the sidelines because we think others know what we're good at. Disorganizers speak their truth, for others to understand.

60: Cultivate Curiosity

In the social age we have multiple, divergent and emergent narratives, and we have billions of data points, facts, and opinions to sift through.

In order to make sense of it all and determine the pathway forward, we need to ask difficult questions and cultivate a dangerous curiosity.

Why dangerous?

Because sniffing around new topics, stepping on others' toes, asking "*Why?*" and "*What if...?*" is courageous work!

We are not certain what understanding will emerge or the direction it will take us. It is exciting, maybe a little scary too.

However, the alternative is more dangerous - to follow others, blindly. To be given someone else's perspective, uncertain if it is grounded in fact or conspiracy.

Curiosity is not just about creativity. It is about finding solid ground on which to stand as all around you shudders.

Disorganize yourself before someone else does it for you.

61: Rocky Balboa

I am a huge fan of the Rocky movie franchise. Stallone really nails the hero's journey through battle, failure and redemption. The intrapreneur in me feels his pain, and the sweetly melancholic victory.

By *Rocky VI*, the protagonist may have had some brain damage, but boy, can he still deliver a punch(line).

Speaking with his fed up, defeatist kid, Rocky hits him with the best piece of advice about working on change I have heard[16]:

> *"Let me tell you something you already know…"*

he exhorts.

> *"It's about how hard you can get hit and keep moving forward; how much you can take and keep moving forward…You gotta be willing to take the hits."*

Change is happening at an increasing rate all around us. Intrapreneurs need to bulk up, and react emotionally to the challenge.

Keep fighting.

62: Embrace Ambiguity

If you are curious, if you are a learner and willing to change and to grow, you are asking lots of questions.

The questions you ask are not the simple ones. They are open-ended, and the answers you get back will be challenging, contradictory.

Good questions do not deliver clarity and certainty. Indeed, quite the opposite. Your investigations will be full of shadow, a grey zone of ambiguity.

This is the world where all the fun happens. Where work is spontaneous; sketched, non-routine, in perpetual beta, following patterns and **insights**.

Ambiguity puts us on full alert and opens up surprises. This is when we achieve breakthrough, this is where the epiphanies occur.

Do not ask for certainty from anyone, do not expect it anywhere.

Intrapreneurs embrace ambiguity. We are always at the edge, always on our toes, senses lit up, ready to respond and to act.

63: Get Rid Of Titles

The number one challenge for talented people at work is that their talent does not match their title or job description.

We are talking about creating the role that manifests your genius. It is unlikely the company will decree it. You need to make it happen.

Let's take charge of the situation and get rid of your title.

A few ways to do this:

get your company to "unboss" the hierarchy, and you apply for project roles and move laterally and vertically with ease. Rare.

Or, give yourself a title that better represents your value and intent.

(*cough* disorganizer, *cough* intrapreneur...)

If it gets a bit clichéd to call yourself *Chief Energizer Bunny*, then you can go for something more generic, that obfuscates the place in the hierarchy but shows the skill set:

Strategy - Project Management - Finance Leader, etc.

Finally, something I see more often on LinkedIn: a brief story. Like,

"I grow companies from stealth to market launch."

Change the org, change the title, or change the story. Disorganize. Act.

64: Under The Stairs

Working out loud is the process by which you make your work:
>   observable; and
>   narrated.

I first started working out loud online. Eventually, I built enough confidence to make it a physical undertaking.

I moved my desk under the stairs in the office. I made myself, as well as my work, visible, observable. People wandering to and fro the office kitchen would chance upon me there.

To make the project unequivocal, I connected a projector to my laptop and broadcast my work against the wall.

Then, for narration, for one week I advertised twice daily Pecha Kucha presentations on the enterprise social network, and invited colleagues to drop by and chat about a miscellaneous topic.

It made me vulnerable, but also available and connected. I had at least 15 unexpected conversations that week with colleagues.

Disorganizers are visible.

Where are you doing your work?

65: Pick Up The Lingo

Be careful of organizational swear words.

(Maybe it's "*Agile!*" or "*Disruption!*").

The kind of words that are always used with quotation marks and a roll of the eyes.

Instead, listen hard for the organizational words and ideas that matter, that have the ear of the bigwigs.

What header appeared a lot in the last strategy plan?
Does the CEO have a go-to call-to-action?
Scan the website for values and phrases that the BD guys are using to differentiate the brand.

Then use them.

(Hey, maybe it's "*Agile!*" or "*Disruption!*" :))

Turn them into weapons for your own intrapreneurial tendencies.

They won't know what hit them.

66: Explain Yourself

Resumes suck, and Aline Lerner[17] has the data to prove, concluding:

> *"at the end of the day, the resume is a low-signal document."*

No doubt. A list of where you worked, the titles you held, the qualifications you earned. Very one-dimensional.

What, then, is the high-signal mechanism for understanding an applicant (or indeed, any network participant)?

Turns out, explaining what you do has the biggest correlation with connecting with the right people.

According to Lerner, on your resume or CV, or cover letter, this means

> *"a concise description of something you worked on recently that you are excited to talk about, as explained to a non-technical audience."*

This is working out loud. Sharing your work openly, attracting interested others towards you. Allowing others to assist.

Intrapreneurs get people to *"Yes!"*

67: Learning Is Public

Learning should not be part of a performance management process, privately applied by you and annually discussed between you and your line manager.

Learning should be public.

> "Work is learning and learning is the work,"

says Harold Jarche.

We should share openly, with radical transparency, the purpose of our work; the actions and processes; the learning; the results; and how we show up doing it.

This is how you get a quantum workplace.

And there's more! The learning is two way.

Radical transparency at work places as many responsibilities and demands on those engaging with your personal learning as it does on you.

We can deploy systems and tools to drive this continuous public learning loop: apps or widgets where feedback is everywhere, and available in real time; pulse surveys; scoring systems; 360 reviews.

This is a profound change in the workplace social contract.

(There is no place to hide.)

Disorganizers understand this. We are ready.

68: Manufacture Serendipity

We have hopefully all experienced the wonderful moment of serendipity, where events just seem to naturally coalesce around us with a happy outcome.

Serendipity is often synonymous with "luck" but there is more to it.

We can manufacture serendipity; we can put in place circumstances where "luck" manifests.

A great, famous example: Steve Jobs designed his own offices with a shared toilet block located at the bottom of stairs.

By doing so, he was encouraging seemingly random meetings to occur between people who were not within their default zone of office engagement. Through these chance meetings, random magic happens.

Now, this chapter was definitely written pre-COVID! So what is the digital, virtual version of this?

Townhalls where you ping people into randomly generated break out rooms? A social network that introduces new colleagues to everyone so we can be known?

Don't leave it to chance. Intrapreneurs make it happen.

69: Teach Me Something (I Don't Know)

A few years ago I wrote a post titled *"Teach me something I don't know."*

It was about the question that Google Founder Sergiy Brin apparently asks interviewees[18]. Put on the spot, interviewees

> *"...think for a minute, and then their eyes just light up. And they tell you about something they're passionate about."*

It turns out that many people, every day, go to google and search on that very topic:

> "Teach me something that I don't know."

Because I get hits to my post from search every day of the year.

Isn't that magical? IRL or online, all around us, people are *seeking*.

Whether it's through a search bar, or a webinar, or a question on a social network, or a raised hand in the team meeting, keep seeking more knowledge; keep asking others to teach you.

This is how we disorganize. We learn, grow, see and manifest breakthroughs.

Teach me something I don't know.

70: People Want Holes

There is a quote attributed to the economist Theodore Levitt that I read like an epiphany:

> *"People don't want to buy a quarter-inch drill; they want a quarter-inch hole."*

It is so obvious, yet mind blowing.

It makes us reconsider all the inputs to the work. What is the experience? What is the outcome? What does the participant leave with?

Peter Drucker said:

> The customer rarely buys what the business thinks it's selling. Nobody pays for a 'product'. What is paid for is *satisfaction*.

> The Company might think it sells products or provides services; the customer has a problem or a job to be done.

People don't want drills. They want holes.

Solving the problem suddenly gets way more complicated, and way more interesting too.

Intrapreneurs can use all their skills and tools to win: working backwards, small bets, squeezing the hivemind, their curiosity. Form follows function.

71: Insights Disorganize

When you attend a conference or speaking event, the panelists or keynotes are often introduced as "insightful." Insight is what we seek. That's why we attend.

They have discovered or uncovered or reimagined something and they are going to share with us.

Interestingly, we attend conferences for insight because we don't get it at work.

Why? Because most organizations value predictability, certainty and perfection. And **_insight is disorganizing_**!

Psychologist Gary Klein writes[19]:

> Insight is the opposite of predictable. Insights are disruptive. They come without warning, take forms that are unexpected, and open up unimagined opportunities. _They are disorganizing._
>
> Insights disrupt progress reviews because they reshape tasks and even revise goals.
>
> They carry risks —unseen pitfalls that can get managers in trouble.

Take care one and all!

Do you _really_ want insight and breakthrough? If so, intrapreneurs are here to help.

72: (Echo Chamber)

In the last chapter I talked about insight and its unpredictability and disorganizing effect. This is not a flaw but its built-in advantage.

Insight takes us outside our bubble of orthodoxy; we escape our own echo chamber.

Can we manufacture insight? Perhaps.

Brian Christian, in his book *The Most Human Human*[20] suggests:

> *"we gain the most insight on a question when we take it to the friend, colleague, or mentor of whose reaction and response we are least certain."*

Escape the echo chamber where we already know the response. Cultivate a network of contrarian and disaggregated viewpoints.

Similarly, he says to gain the most insight into a person, we should ask the question of whose answer we're least certain.

Insight requires intentionality.

We are not wandering around chitchatting; we are muscling up in the battle of ideas. We are embracing uncertainty; ready and willing to disorganize.

73: Keep A Peasant's Heart

In my study and learning, I keep coming back to this question:

How do we make a bigger, or the biggest, difference?

It is easy to see ourselves as a tiny cog in The Machine, useful but rarely impactful. Especially for those who are disenfranchised from the decision-making process and the opportunity matrix by systemic barriers to entry: gender, race, socio-economic standing.

This is simply a reminder - that it is possible, it is plausible, that **you are the one to make it happen.**

There is a line in *Ulysses* by James Joyce that holds that space of possibility:

"The movements which work revolutions in the world are born out of the dreams and visions in a peasant's heart on a hillside."

More poetic and idealistic than anything I could craft, but you can change the world!

To disorganize your workplace is to start something, somewhere. Small and unnoticed at first, but with a rippling effect that amplifies and scales over time and through others.

74: *What If...?*

There are four stages of design thinking.

It begins with *"What is"* - the present state in which we find ourselves, the situation or initiative.

It then moves to *"What if...?"* where we envision a new, improved future.

"What wows" comes next, focused on solutions that stand out.

Finally, *"What works"* tests possible solutions with users in the real world.

Could there be a more beautiful question than *"what if..?"*

It is a sentence that is often prefaced with

> *"Ooooh...! What if...?"*

It activates the imagination, it releases endorphins.

"What is..." and *"what works..."* ground the investigation in reality, they round out the corners, but without imagining a different, better tomorrow, what's the point?

Intrapreneurs keep imagining *"What if...?"*

75: Hiring Advice

We often get hiring and promotions back to front.

We look for people with existing experience doing the role, because we approach the process risk adversely, with the idea that we will therefore minimize errors.

Rather, we should approach from a place of possibility.

The founder of Visa, Dee Hock has the best hiring advice of all.

He says it starts with integrity and ends in experience, because...

> "Without integrity, motivation is dangerous;
> without motivation, capacity is impotent;
> without capacity, understanding is limited;
> without understanding, knowledge is meaningless;
> without knowledge, experience is blind.
> Experience is easy to provide and quickly put to good use by people with all the other qualities."

Seek out the unknown, the unexpected, the dreamers and misfits, the unheralded. The disorganizers.

76: (The Answer Is) Yes

There is a beautiful and discombobulating quote from the famous composer Leonard Bernstein, which goes like this:

"I am no longer sure of the question, but I am certain of the answer: YES!"

This really speaks to me.

One of my biggest motivations at work is to engender a *"YES!"* from my audience.

I spent too many years at work thinking it was about getting through the day, keeping everything on an even keel. It was much later when I realized individual workers could create breakthrough actions, initiatives and outcomes.

If we want to lead, and if you want that leadership to be about more and making a bigger difference, then you need colleagues to say

"Yes!"

- to change, to the emergent, to the disorganized next.

Aim high, go big. Get to Yes!

77: Yes. And....

Last chapter, I beseeched you all to go for *"Yes!"* Get the crowd cheering and hollering. High fives all round.

What's another way to look at this idea?

Let's consider the basic rule of improv theatre:

Yes. And...

The experience of improv is one of unexpected outcomes. The joining of the dots between two seemingly irrelevant concepts to create a whole new, delightful narrative.

This unexpectedness emerges from an almost irrational willingness to go with the flow.

Usually, and especially at work, our brain is set to RATIONAL mode.

I say "X", you consider X and all its facets and offer a counter argument or position:

> *"Yes* (we are colleagues and on the same team), *but...* (you have not thought it through correctly and my role is to course correct.)"

"Yes. And..." says something different.

"Yes (you are exactly what is required). *And...*(what if I pushed your thinking even further!?) "

The intrapreneur is a *"Yes! And..."* friend, confidant, and supporter.

78: Ask Questions

This chapter is about the theme tune of the kids' TV animation Bob the Builder[21] -

>   *"Can we fix it? Yes we can!"*

A test group of people is asked to repeat twenty times over:

>   "I can fix it!"

Then they are given problems to 'fix.'

Another test group is asked to repeat this sentence twenty times:

>   "Can I fix it?"

Then they are given the same problems to 'fix.'

Which group does best in the problem-solving? If you said: the group which is reflective and questioning, questing and open-minded, you are CORRECT! Congratulations.

Pondering a problem, perhaps with the possibility that you might not succeed, gets to better outcomes than declaring definitively that you will get there.

This is the art of being a fixer, an intrapreneur. Ask good questions - of yourself and others - rather than making assertions.

You have to live in the uncertainty that you might fail; but doing so means, you are less likely to!

79: Relentless Humanity

Over the last decade I have been relentlessly learning, growing, changing, and challenging.

It is hard work, driven by the need to keep my skills fresh, and deal with an ever-changing technological and stakeholder landscape.

Relentless means never-ending, incessant. It carries with it a heavy weight, it tires. But we must keep on going, moving forward, learning, unlearning, relearning. We just must.

To balance this intent, I keep bringing my thinking back to people, about the impacts on colleagues and stakeholders, for good and bad.

Humanity.

Because when you see someone whole, you see the pros and cons, the good and bad, the genius and the foibles, and it is all ok. You accept them, humbly, and they you.

Work is human; and it is *humane.*

Pandemics and working from home and Zoom calls may be driving organizational change in 2020, but that is not the thing that really matters.

Disorganizers stand directly in front of another, arms wide, hopeful, asking:

> *How can I help?*

80: Ahead Of Your Time

The provocateur Ted Rubin once said,

"Being called 'ahead of your time' means you failed."

I think about this often. In times where *'disruption'* and *'innovation'* are watchwords for success, we are always looking to move forward and ahead of the pack.

Generally, it is an ideal I subscribe to, but there should be caution in our sprints. How far we are ahead, and what we are doing to bring people towards us, is critical to consider.

Intrapreneurship is about making change, not just recognizing it. We see it, convey the need to others, and add the operational steps to make the market ready.

It is not enough to just inject creative tension; nor to get in your own flow about the topic. You need to hustle new outcomes too.

81: People Before Potatoes

I deployed my first cloud technology solution 10 years ago, to replace an old, creaking piece of tech.

In that process, I created second order effects.

> IT jumped into the twenty-first century.
> The leadership team jumped a generation or two in how they connected with colleagues.
> Alongside a cohort of similar evangelists, we proselytized a new future of corporate tech, one that created big problems for ourselves as our organizations creaked under the change we delivered.

I learned a big lesson:

> Do not be the agent for technology change.

It gets the whole learning and change process back to front. Be, instead, the agent for people – colleagues, friends, partners – to live a better (work) tomorrow.

In *Life, The Universe, And Everything*, Douglas Adams presciently advises,

> *"It is a mistake to think you can solve any major problems just with potatoes."*

It is a message for the intrapreneur. People before potatoes.

82: Meander More

I used to spend a lot of time lying on my sofa staring at the ceiling. I had a girlfriend, who was always busy, who would ask me

"What are you doing?"

to which I would answer,

"Nothing."

Only it was everything. A journey around my mind, conjuring thoughts and ideas, scraps of memories and possible future outcomes. Shapes and patterns would emerge; epiphanies came a'callin'. I was time travelling.

In neuroscience, this mind wandering is referred to as the brain's state of REST, or Random Episodic Silent Thought.

It is your brain's most delicious gift, if we give it the opportunity. To *meander*.

However, this gift is under attack - by our mobile devices[22]. When we have a super computer in hand, there is too much to focus on. We have less cognitive downtime. We commit less time to travelling around our mind.

This is a threat.

Disorganizers benefit from having nothing to do.

Put down your phone, and stare at the ceiling more.

83: Curiosity And Focus Are Antagonistic

I watched a speech[23] by Jonny Ive from Apple about the challenge of matching *curiosity* - seeking new learning; and *focus* - the execution of tasks to move forward.

Curiosity and focus are in antagonism - they repel and feed off each other.

They are two sides of the same coin.

This is a useful dichotomy to reflect on:
- curiosity drives ideas;
- ideas lead to breakthrough thinking in the resolution of problems.
- Solving problems, though, requires focus, attention and hard work;
- whereas curiosity can lead one down blind alleys, or in circles.
- Without purpose, curiosity is unfulfilled.
- Both are intertwined, feeding off each other, although they are opposites.

My default start point is curiosity. But give me a problem to solve and I will work on it with velocity to quickly get to action.

Intrapreneurs try to find a balance.

84: Be a Disagreeable Giver

The organizational psychologist Adam Grant[24] talks about a personality matrix on two axes: *givers and takers*, and *agreeable and disagreeable*.

We can imagine that colleagues who *take* are a nightmare to work with, selfish and focused on their own needs.

But what about the degree of *agreeableness* in colleagues? Grant says the friendly, agreeable givers are averse to conflict. It can be too easy...

Disagreeable givers are the most valuable.

They are a pain in the ass, but fight for what they believe in, challenge the status quo, push for painful, necessary change, they avoid complacency. Their grouchy disposition means when they praise something, it can be trusted.

Intrapreneurship is all about challenging the existing order and willing to do the work to make things better. Disagreeable givers...

85: Small Pieces, Loosely Joined

Dave Weinberger co-wrote the *Cluetrain Manifesto*, which introduced us to the network economy, through which disorganizers emerge from the hierarchy in their power.

Weinberger also wrote a book about a unified theory of the web called *Small Pieces, Loosely Joined*, but really, it is a book about society, about community. It talks of hope and time and togetherness. It is about big things said simply.

"Small pieces, loosely joined" should be a mantra of the disorganizer.

We are trying to change the world when we do not necessarily have the decision-making power to do so.

We need to experiment and iterate and create intimate victories. We remix existing ideas from our network. We do it with fellow travellers, from across the organization and from without. We learn together and from each other and spur each other on to greatness.

No massive, noble goal. Just small pieces, loosely joined...

86: Sticky Notes

In the last chapter I discussed small pieces, loosely joined.

We don't need a single methodology to act and make a difference. We need to move out in multiple directions and join the dots as we go. How do we do this?

Here's one simple way: get out your colourful sticky notes and some sharpie pens, and gather together a group of fellow travellers to brainstorm.

The world does not work in a linear fashion. We remix existing work in new ways. Emergence is a guiding light. Take a tough, gnarly topic and reimagine it.

Write lots of top-of-mind, esoteric ideas on post-it notes and throw them on the wall. Stand back and let the data wash over you.

Then step forward and start transforming and combining the data. Try unusual combinations, surprise yourself and others.

Be a little crazy. Move to the edge of your comfort zone.

Experiment. Disorganize.

87: Act. Sense. Change.

You are asked to drive a new initiative in the org - new tech, behaviours, community practices.

You seek adoption.

But!

People are change averse. So here comes the change management plan, which educates and directs.

However, 80% of change programs fail (see *80:20*); and 90% of everything is crap (see *Sturgeon's Law*)!

Change Agent Simon Terry[25] has another idea. He suggests we get to change through action. As we act, we sense what is working and how, and change is the natural outcome.

It is a generous, enabling and trust building approach. Understanding what you are trying to achieve, you *"act as if..."* and in so doing you create change in the culture.

As Terry says,

> "Others see the practice and the benefits and are encouraged to copy and reinforce them. Over time this consistent practice and the community it builds does more to change the organization than posters, videos and CEO speeches."

Amen. Intrapreneurs take action. They use their sense-making skills to observe and review. They make change happen.

88: Storytelling Brings Curiosity To Life

I happen to be a communicator, and therefore storytelling is a core skill set and process in how I go about my business.

It should be yours too, no matter your profession.

If you are curious and a learner, you will undertake many experiments and make many mistakes, just as you will experience breakthrough and epiphany.

Those lessons are reminders to you, and useful to others. They ground the work in reality. A reality that others can imagine and own for themselves.

Brian Glazer, author of *A Curious Mind* says,

"the story is a report from the front lines of curiosity."

Storytelling is the act of bringing home the discoveries learned.

Share is the new save, it is our default position. Disorganizers share their stories - wins and losses - to support others and to activate their curiosity and enable their discoveries.

Rinse and repeat.

89: Thinking Advantage

Why do you do the things you do?

You should have some ideas about this! Speed without direction doesn't get you anywhere except a crash.

How do you do the things you do?

You should have some philosophy about this too. Some guiding principles about how you show up, so others can orient around you and support.

These ideas should be codified. *Write them down*.

Call them a manifesto or not, this list, whether shared or hidden in your journal (or your head) is your own call to action, where your individual genius can make (all) the difference. It allows others to know you; and to ask for your help.

- Decide what is important to change
- Select the right topic
- Start conversing
- Write it down!
- Act according to it
- Refine it
- Pair it to your skills
- Create some guiding principles
- Start a movement around it
- Organize and execute.

This manifesto is the intrapreneur's thinking advantage[26].

90: Hustle & Flow

Hustle has a negative connotation these days, but I like to see it as forward momentum, making things happen.

Today's society waits for no woman. Tomorrow's may walk all over us. We need to light a fire – we need to move faster. Hustle says,

> *"Get a move on!"*

Also, like the cockroach, the hustler may be the only one to survive the apocalypse!

Flow is the counterpart. In flow, we are open-minded, prepared, learning, growing. We accept the support of others, picking up speed and absorbing energy.

Mihaly Csikszentmihalyi calls flow,

> *"an intense focus and crisp sense of clarity where you forget yourself, lose track of time, and feel like you're part of something larger."*

Flow can seem a little touchy-feely, so I like to marry it with hustle, to create the tension.

In combination, these two attributes are unstoppable, and the disorganizer will be too.

91: Trust

How does a network of people who are unrelated, who have never met, where there is no commercial prearrangement, work?

The best results arrive when people approach the network with an open mind and an open heart, participating with the expectation that others will do likewise.

(This is similar to the Prisoner's Dilemma concept.)

Successful networks showcase that we need to learn (or relearn) to trust others. If you are sceptical of this idea, you will not survive the future of work.

More poignantly, I realize, this trust starts with ourselves[27]. We must learn to trust that our own participation adds value within the network. If you are scared of this idea, you need to get over yourself.

We need to move toward others, arms out wide, asking

> *"How can I help?"*

If we do this, there will be people on the other side of the embrace; people who will reciprocate. Disorganizers must trust.

92: Be FRESH

Corporate life can confine. It is like a straitjacket.

Everything is so *serious*. Professionalism has sucked the life out of the human experience of work.

We should fight back; seek to inject a tiny piece of humanity into our work whenever we can.

My own approach is to *be F.R.E.S.H.: fun, revealing, entertaining, shareable & social, heartfelt.*

FRESH is a mantra for me, to remind myself that I live in a person-to-person economy. We must connect at the individual level; and build out from there networks of humans.

This is *my* approach. Find your own.

It does not matter what ethos you have, but make it real and honest; and make it so that others can accept it and embrace it for themselves.

If you want to succeed in your intrapreneurial intent, others need to say "*Yes!*" too.

93: Connect. Everything. Is Connected.

When we disorganize our company, we are often noodling on small ideas and unobtrusive experiments. We want to fail forward without worry, and we join the dots as we go.

However, it cannot be simply a random, scattergun set of actions.

We need some unifying theme around which we orient and through which we tell a great institutional story - for others to say "*Yes!*" to us.

My themes are around community and culture, about activating individuals for more, to scale the organizational whole.

In that thematic pursuit, I seek to *connect everything*. I am joining the dots. Those individual actions and experiments add up to something greater than the sum of the parts.

At the same time, I practice a form of organizational spirituality. I believe that *everything is connected*. We are in service of something bigger than the individual tasks.

Working from small to large, large to small gives the intrapreneur flexibility and scope.

94: Everyone Needs a Studio 20

Our creative agency work was almost entirely in-house. The team did it all: strategy, writing, graphics, audio, video, 360, podcasts, editing, all the post-production. We had equipment everywhere, always a handful of cameras and mics and lights to hand.

The office manager asked us to kindly tidy it all away, and at the end of a corridor of sliding bookshelf storage we found a small space that was ours and ours alone - and created Studio 20.

(It was on the 20th floor...)

A place where we could imagine, craft, and produce our work.

Everyone needs a studio 20:
      of the *body* – a location to call your own; or
      of the *mind* – a place of escape and release, a place of protection and safety.

Where is that place you can call your own to disorganize?

A whiteboard, the spare bedroom, the office cafeteria, Friday afternoon when all the work is completed...?

Find a place called home.

95: What We Know Will Change

I read a review of Richard Power's Pulitzer-winning novel *The Overstory*, an interlocking narrative of different people and times and places, in which the reviewer noted

> *"the only thing consistent is the seeking – and the humility to understand that we will change."*

Yes.

If I think I can share something of value, if I consider that my actions might make the world a better place, I do so with this in mind:

> Things change, people change, organizations change.

What works today might not tomorrow, whether it is my good idea of yours. We must always be ready to go again, to rework the initiative, to spin up an even better idea.

What is important is that we keep seeking - the more, the next, the better.

The seeker is the person who discovers the future. The seeker is an intrapreneur.

96: How Novel!

You, in your enthusiasm and wide-eyed excitement, have a *"What if…"* moment and explain your idea to your leader.

>*"What a novel idea!"*

comes the agnostic reply.

You know that idea is in trouble, or that you work for the wrong leader.

In his book, *Seeing What Others Don't,* Gary Klein notes research that found that if an idea is novel, people automatically assume it isn't practical or reliable. Novel ideas are associated with failures.

>*"Creativity was connected with uncertainty and generally, managers dislike uncertainty and unpredictability, and therefore distrust creativity. "*

Ugh.

This "perfection trap" is debilitating to breakthrough thinking and actions. As Klein notes, encouraging insights becomes limited to

>*"hanging inspirational posters on the walls."*

Ouch.

Intrapreneurs choose their leaders and organizations wisely.

97: Flâneur

A flâneur is defined as

> *the person of leisure, the idler, the urban explorer, the connoisseur of the street.*

What strikes me is how apropos is the flâneur's approach to the world in the here and now.

Observant, immersed, knowledgeable and acknowledging everything around them.

The flâneur is of the people, networked in the community, able to navigate the ebb and flow of ideas, theories, and forces around them. Controlled, yet intrigued.

What a thoroughly modern skillset and approach to the amorphous world we inhabit.

Participatory but not carried away; aware but never dogmatic; full of delight rather than zeal. A clear eye on the world, with one foot in.

Curious, undaunted, ready to disorganize.

It's a flâneur's life for me.

98: ← This Much We Know →

I named my practice after an article that has run in *The Observer* newspaper for years, *This Much I Know*[28]. Famous people share their learnings, large and small.

I find it very inviting, open and kind.

I want to channel that in my own work.

I changed the "*I*" to "*We*" because I have been on a shared journey with colleagues, network friends and mentors. I steal from others ahead, and seek to pass it on to those just behind or alongside.

I make no promises about knowing everything.

But I do make a promise that in my place of excellence, working in my wheelhouse, spewing up my genius...by gad, I'm good at some stuff...This is how I disorganize.

Outside of that, well, I suggest you make no promises, except that you **stretch yourself towards everything.**

This Much We Know.

99: Smash The Like Button

This series of notes has been easy to execute because of the hard graft I have put into my practice over the last decade plus. Many of the chapters write themselves because I wear the experiences in my bones.

I share these lessons not because I think I am particularly special or unique - there are many, many people who work at a higher standard of execution and insight.

I share because that is the gift I can offer. Over the years, people have encouraged me to push for more, and to share the learnings.

My request for you is that you do the same.

At work, how often can you stare at your audience directly in the eye, and demand they

SMASH THE LIKE BUTTON?!

Those times that you have, and that they did...hold those moments.

Replicate them. Enhance them. Go for more.

Disorganize better than ever. Share your 99 intrapreneurial tips and tricks.

Let's take this whole thing forward.

Acknowledgements

To those who showed me what can be achieved through hard work, net work, resilience, humour, expertise, reflection, creativity and kindness; and who encouraged and pushed me:

Oscar, Kelvin, Sean, Paul, Alex, Tarik and the FS/BB team; Lois, Jim, Kingsley, Priscilla, Solomon, Denisa, Lillian, Angelique, Lisa, Axel, Melissa, Peter and the TK crew; Bart; Jordan; Susan, Lois, Harold, Jon, Simon, Catherine, Joachim, Celine, Dany, Christoph, Marcia, Rob, Dennis, and all the CAWW family; the Yammer CRMs and all the inspirational fellow travellers in my social business network from whom I have learned.

Footnotes

[1] http://www.fastcoexist.com/3015652/futurist-forum/8-new-jobs-people-will-have-in-2025
[2] Entrepreneurship: https://www.economist.com/business/2013/07/20/crazy-diamonds
[3] DDOs: https://thismuchweknow.net/2017/01/06/12-measures-of-a-deliberately-developmental-organization-ddo/
[4] Follow Cindy on each and every channel you can: www.twitter.com/cindygallop
[5] Lois Kelly: https://twitter.com/LoisKelly/
[6] https://twitter.com/AdamMGrant/status/1009143733818941440
[7] Harold Jarche: https://jarche.com/2012/06/work-is-learning-and-learning-is-the-work/
[8] https://seths.blog/2011/03/reject-the-tyranny-of-being-picked-pick-yourself/
[9] https://thismuchweknow.net/2013/05/16/the-edge-is-the-new-core/
[10] Kirby Ferguson: https://twitter.com/remixeverything
[11] Luis Suarez: www.twitter.com/elsua
[12] www.ChangeAgentsWorldwide.com
[13] http://www.bakadesuyo.com/2014/09/how-to-get-respect/
[14] https://thismuchweknow.net/2016/09/15/working-backwards-to-outcomes/
[15] https://thismuchweknow.net/2013/04/04/4-manifestos-to-live-by-4-incomplete-manifesto-for-growth/
[16] https://thismuchweknow.net/2013/11/20/everything-i-learned-about-change-i-learned-from-rocky-balboa/
[17] http://thismuchweknow.net/2015/02/25/working-out-loud-is-a-high-signal-approach-to-understanding-and-heres-the-data/
[18] https://www.fastcompany.com/3007369/heres-google-perk-any-company-can-imitate-employee-employee-learning
[19] https://www.psychologytoday.com/ca/blog/seeing-what-others-dont/201307/insights-vs-organizations
[20] http://www.amazon.com/Most-Human-Talking-Computers-Teaches/dp/0385533063
[21] Bob the Builder: https://www.youtube.com/watch?v=n8YWZm_YKoo
[22] https://www.nytimes.com/interactive/2018/11/15/magazine/tech-design-ai-prediction.html
[23] https://9to5mac.com/2018/11/20/jony-ive-discusses-the-importance-and-absurdity-between-leveraging-curiosity-and-the-focus-to-solve-problems/
[24] https://qz.com/work/1309735/adam-grant-the-best-employees-are-not-the-agreeable-ones/
[25] Simon Terry: https://www.linkedin.com/pulse/collaboration-adoption-act-your-way-new-thinking-simon-terry
[26] https://thismuchweknow.net/2015/02/02/why-do-you-need-your-own-manifesto-because-they-get-you-to-action/
[27] https://thismuchweknow.net/2014/01/28/i-must-relearn-to-trust/
[28] https://www.theguardian.com/lifeandhealth/series/thismuchiknow

About The Author

Jonathan Anthony has spent a 20-year+ intrapreneurial career working for multinational consumer and energy companies on three continents, at the intersection of marketing and corporate communications, culture, brand, technology transformation, and organizational effectiveness.

His learning and practice is often categorised under the term *Social Business*; about which, amongst other topics, he regularly blogs on www.ThisMuchWeKnow.net. He is a Charter Member of *Change Agents Worldwide*. He helps clients through the *This Much We Know* consultancy, where he channels his personal brand promises: *Be FRESH*; and *Encourage, Act, Reimagine*.

Made in the USA
Coppell, TX
24 November 2024

40888058R00067